Approaches to writing and language
BOOK 3

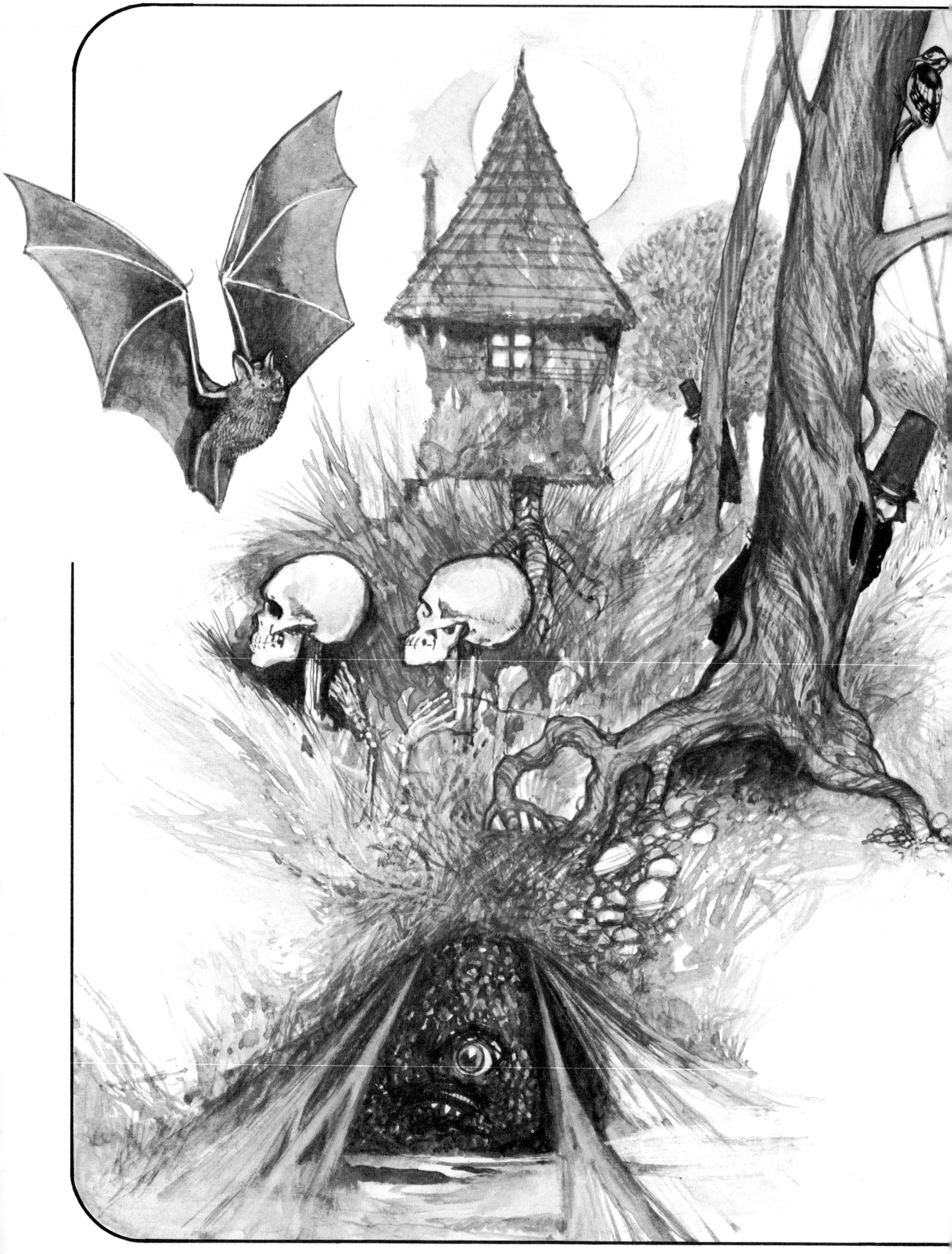

Sheila Lane
& Marion Kemp

Approaches to writing and language
BOOK 3

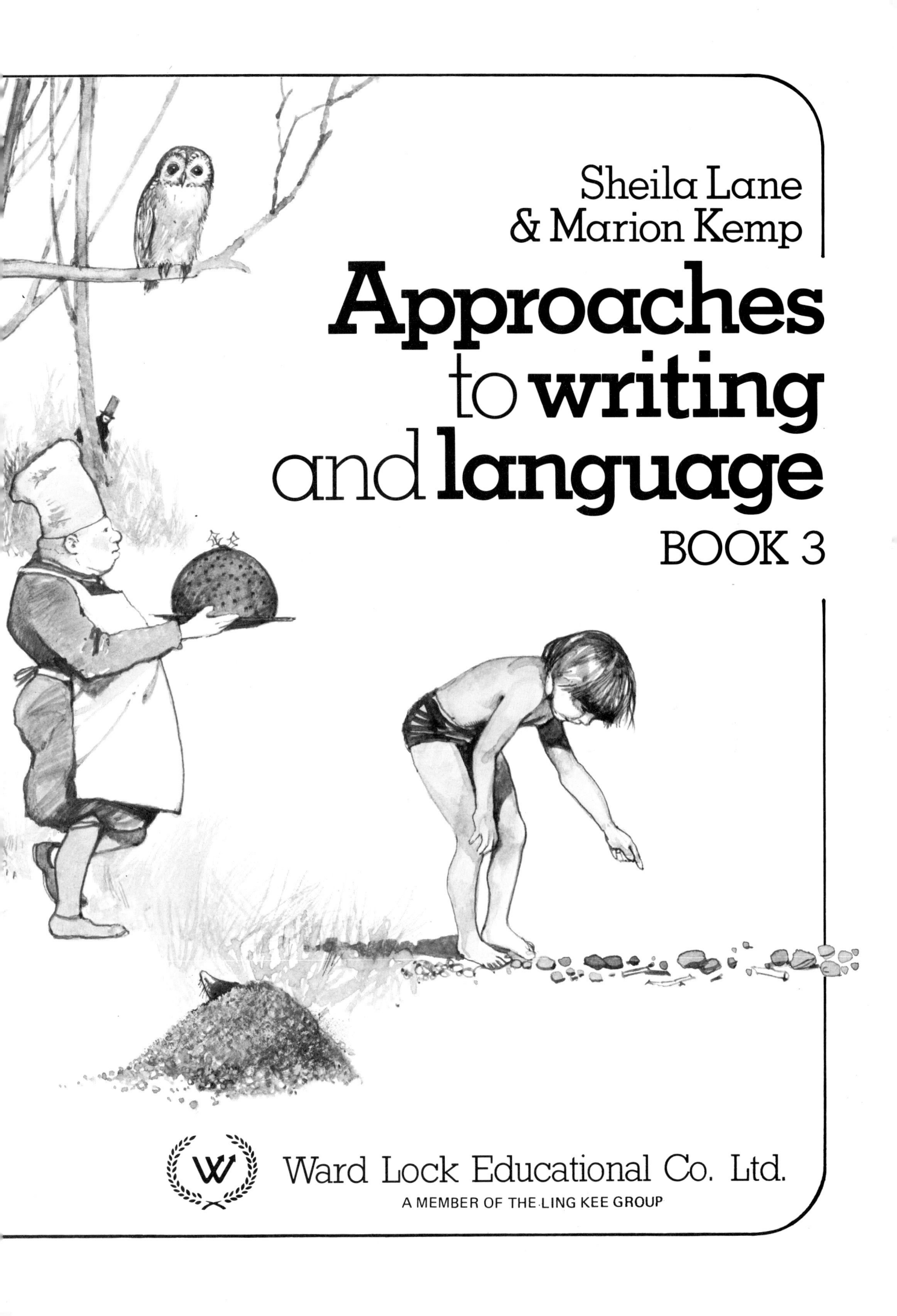

Ward Lock Educational Co. Ltd.
A MEMBER OF THE LING KEE GROUP

WARD LOCK EDUCATIONAL CO. LTD.
T.R. House, 1 Christopher Road
East Grinstead, Sussex RH19 3BT

A member of the Ling Kee Group
LONDON · HONG KONG · NEW YORK · SINGAPORE

© Marion Kemp and Sheila Lane 1980

All rights reserved. No part of this publication may be reproduced, stored in a retrieval system or transmitted in any form, or by any means, electronic, mechanical, photocopying, recording or otherwise, without the prior permission of the copyright owner.

First published 1981
Reprinted 1981, 1982, 1985, 1986, 1987, 1989

Designed by Clare Osborn
Illustrated by David Mostyn and Tony Morris
Set in 14 point Futura and Stymie

Approaches to Writing and Language
Book 1   0 7062 3926 1
Book 2   0 7062 3927 X
Book 3   0 7062 3928 8
Book 4   0 7062 3929 6

Printed in Hong Kong

Contents

Inside me _____ 6
The extraordinary thing _____ 8
Who's in there? _____ 10
Shape poems _____ 13
Friends or enemies? _____ 14
Story building _____ 16
Before and after _____ 19
Letter writing _____ 20
Pudding time _____ 22
What's inside? _____ 24
Using your eyes _____ 28
Picture poems _____ 30
Which one would you choose? _____ 32
The fire bird _____ 36
Fire! Fire! _____ 39
Tracking and trailing _____ 42
What do you see? _____ 44
What do you think? _____ 48
A great invention _____ 50
Can you solve it? _____ 53
Animal lives _____ 54
The naming of plants _____ 58
Strange places _____ 60
Making a holiday choice _____ 62

Inside me

Do you ever sit and daydream?
What goes on inside your head when you should be concentrating?

'Miss Barter thinks I'm reading
But...'

I'm taming lions

I'm on the moon

I'm having a fight with an octopus

'Miss Barter thinks I'm listening
But no...'

I'm diving off a cliff

I'm boxing for the navy

I'm sitting and floating in a big balloon

All the ideas on page 6 come from a poem
by Richard Crompton, aged ten.

Richard wrote his poem like this:

Day Dreams

Miss Barter thinks I'm reading
But I'm taming lions,
or stalking kangaroos . . .
I'm on the moon . . .
or swimming under water.
I have a fight with an octopus
and a giant sword fish . . .
Miss Barter thinks I'm listening —
But no.
I'm boxing for the navy . . .
I'm diving off a cliff . . .
I sit and float
in a big balloon
soaring through the clouds,
floating swiftly.

Notebook

Think about what you would like to be doing **now**.
Make a list of your ideas.
Begin each idea with: I'm . . . or: I am . . .

Writing

Write you own poem, using ideas from your list.
You could use the name of your own teacher or someone in your family
instead of 'Miss Barter'.
Read your poem to yourself and decide on the **one** thing
you would like to do **most of all**.

Writing

Write a short piece called: *Most of All*
You could write about: where you would like to be —
whether you would like to be with other people or alone —
why you want this so much.

The extraordinary thing

Read these four paragraphs which begin a story
called: *The Bunyip of Berkeley's Creek*

> Late one night, for no particular reason, something stirred in the black mud at the bottom of Berkeley's Creek.

> The fish swam away in fright, and the night birds in the trees hid their heads under their wings.

> When they looked again, something very large and very muddy was sitting on the bank.

> 'What am I?' it murmured. 'What am I, what am I, what am I?' And the night birds quickly hid their heads under their wings again.

Notebook

Write these sentences with the correct endings
from the story called: *The Bunyip of Berkeley's Creek.*

. . . late one night.
All this happened . . . early in the morning.
. . . at twelve o'clock, midnight.

. . . in the green slime.
Something stirred . . . in the squishy-squashy slush.
. . . in the black mud.

. . . swam behind the water weeds.
The fish . . . swam around in circles.
. . . swam away in fright.

. . . squawked noisily and flew away.
The night birds . . . hid their heads under their wings.
. . . blinked sleepily and closed their eyes.

. . . sitting on the bank.
Something was . . . squatting on a tree stump.
. . . clinging to a large rock.

. . . croaked, 'Where am I?'
The Thing . . . murmured, 'What am I?'
. . . stuttered, 'Wh-wh-wh-o - am I?'

Before you write your story

Read all the sentences again.
Find a set of sentences to begin a new story about *Another Extraordinary Thing.*
Read the set of sentences you have chosen, over and over again to yourself.
Make a picture in your mind of this new extraordinary thing.

Writing

Write your own story. You could call your writing: *Another Extraordinary Thing*
What will your Extraordinary Thing turn out to be?

Other ideas

Did you know that one blue whale weighs 480 lions or 4,800,000 mice?
Did you know that it takes 40 minutes to hard boil an ostrich egg?
      . . . a cheetah can run at 135 km an hour?
      . . . a golfer can hit a ball through 500 pages of a telephone directory?
You could make your own collection of *Extraordinary Facts.*

Who's in there?

Read this description of the **outside** of an extraordinary place.

The fence round the post was made of human bones, and on the fence posts there were skulls, glaring out of their eye sockets. And instead of the gate there were feet, instead of bolts there were hands, instead of the lock there was a mouth with sharp teeth. And inside the fence there was a little hut standing on a cock's foot and turning round and round.

Could the hut be the home of a witch, a demon, a ghost, or...?

Look again at the picture. Can you see: the two skulls, the gate of bony fingers, dangling bare bones, grinning teeth, the revolving cock's foot?
Think of a frightening name for the extraordinary place in the picture.

Writing

You could use the frightening name as a title for your writing.
Write a short piece to describe: *This Extraordinary Place called...*

Read this description of the **inside** of another unusual place:

There were stones and bones, fossils and bottles, skins and tins, stacks of sticks and hanks of string. There were motor-car tyres and hats from old scarecrows, nuts and bolts and bobbles from brass bedsteads. There was a coal scuttle full of dead electric light bulbs and a basin with rusty screws and nails in it. There was a pile of bracken and newspapers that looked as if it were used for a bed.

Think about how this strange collection of odds and ends got into the den.
Who or what might live there?
Could the den have been hidden in a pit, or a quarry, or a cave, or . . . ?

A boy called Barney knew where there was a chalk pit.

The sides of the pit were white chalk,
with lines of flints poking out in places . . .
Far below was the bottom of the pit. The dump.
Barney could see strange bits of wreckage
among the moss and elder bushes and nettles.
Was that the steering wheel of a ship?
The tail of an aeroplane . . . ?

Think about the kind of place you would choose for a hide-away.
Would it be: an old house, an empty cave, a deserted warehouse,
a ruined barn, thick bushes, or . . . ?
Make a list of all the odds and ends you would collect for your secret place.

Writing

Write a short piece about: *My Hidden Den*

In this short extract, the description of the **inside** of the Space Craft has been left out.

> The gigantic sausage-shaped capsule was no less than one thousand feet long.
> It was called Space Hotel U.S.A. and it was the marvel of the Space Age.
> It had inside . . .
> It was fully air-conditioned. It was also equipped with a gravity-making machine so that you didn't float about inside it. You walked normally.

Think about the inside of a Space Hotel.
How might the bedrooms and bathrooms be arranged?
What kind of recreation rooms might be provided?
Might there be some special Space Sports Competitions?
Think about how food might be served. It might be from:

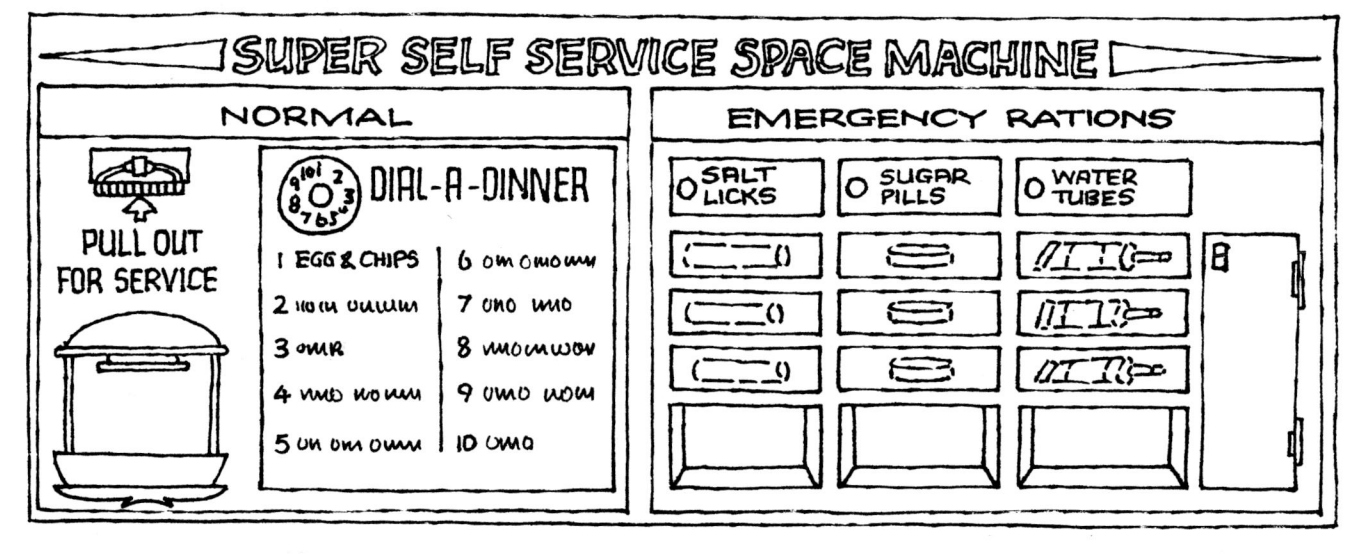

Notebook

Make up 10 different dinners for **Normal**.
Make up some new ideas for **Emergency Rations**.

Writing

Write a short piece about: *Inside Space Hotel*

Write a long story

You have written descriptions of three different places.
Decide which place interests you most and think about an exciting adventure story which you make happen in the place which you have chosen.
Write a long adventure story about: *A Haunted House*
　　　　　　　　　　　　or: *The Mystery of the Hidden Den*
　　　　　　　　　　　　or: *Adventures in Space*

Shape poems

Spike Milligan's poem is written so that the shape of the lines shows the meaning of the words.

Sailor John

Johnny was a sailor lad who sailed the salty sea.
He loved to be on board a ship and feel the wind blo' free!

But then one day a storm blew up. The waves were ten feet high!

'All hands on deck!' The cry went up. 'Or we are doomed to die!'

But Johnny was a sailor brave. 'Don't worry lads,' cried he,

'I'll show you how to save a ship from going down at sea.'

Here is part of a poem by Carl Sandburg.

Write

Write out the poem so that the shape of the lines shows the meaning of the words.

Worms

Worms go down and up and over and under.
Worms like tunnels.
Curve worms never like circle worms.
The shape of a crooked worm satisfies a crooked worm.
A straight worm says, 'Why not be straight?'
Long worms slither farther than short worms.

Friends or enemies

Do you think that these two birds are friends or enemies?

Read the information about the Tawny Owl and the Great Woodpecker.

Tawny Owl	Great Woodpecker
appearance brownish in colour special wing feathers for muffled flight large eyes set to look straight forward **home** uses empty hole in tree left by squirrels or crows **food** small animals e.g. mice and large beetles — tears food apart with hooked beak and sharp claws **sound** screeching sound calls tu-whit tu-whoo, to other birds **behaviour** out at night to hunt for food almost soundless wing beat so it can swoop silently onto prey	**appearance** black and white in colour red feathers on crown of head strong tail feathers used as extra leg when climbing long, sticky tongue tiny hooked bristles on end **home** makes own hole in tree by pecking out wood with beak **food** tiny insects living in bark of tree — pushes special tongue into cracks of tree bark and hooks insects out **sound** hammering sound when pecking out hole for nest calls with a fast drumming sound by tapping beak on wood to other birds out in daytime **behaviour** out in daytime climbs up and down tree using tail feathers as a kind of third leg to keep it steady

The Tawny Owl is usually very **quiet**, but the Great Woodpecker is very **noisy**.

Notebook

Use your dictionary to make a **word chain** of **quiet** words.

(quiet)(soundless)( )( )( )

Use your dictionary to make a **word chain** of **noisy** words.

(noisy)(hammering)( )( )( )

Read the information again about the Tawny Owl and the Great Woodpecker. As you read, think about the **differences** between the two birds.

Write

Write the heading:
Differences between the Tawny Owl and the Great Woodpecker

Work through the information and write sentences about the differences between the two birds like this:

The Tawny Owl is a brownish colour, but the Great Woodpecker is . . .

The Owl sleeps during the day.
Think about how the Woodpecker would disturb it during the day by the hammering of its nest-making and its fast drumming call to the other birds.
When would the Woodpecker be disturbed by the Owl?
Could a conversation between the two birds become an angry argument?

Writing

Write: *An argument between a Tawny Owl and a Great Woodpecker*

You could begin:

Owl　　　What's that? What's that?
　　　　　Is that you again, Woodpecker?

Woodpecker So you've woken up, have you, Owl?
　　　　　Do you realize that at midnight last night you . . .

When the argument becomes very strong, the two birds might make unkind and rude remarks about: each other's appearance, homes, food, habits, etc.

Story building

A **paragraph** is a short passage, or a collection of sentences, which fit together to make a part of a piece of writing.

Read these four paragraphs which begin the story.

The Three Robbers

Once upon a time there were three fierce robbers.
They went about hidden under large black capes and tall black hats.

The first had a blunderbuss. The second had a pepper-blower. The third had a huge red axe.

In the dark of the night they walked the roads, searching for victims. They terrified everyone. Women fainted. Brave men ran. Dogs fled. Carriages stopped when the robbers blew pepper in the horses eyes. With the axe they smashed the carriage wheels. And with the blunderbuss they threatened the passengers and plundered them.

The robbers' hide-out was in a cave high up in the mountains. There they carried their loot. They had trunks full of gold, jewels, money, watches, wedding rings and precious stones.

The first paragraph describes the characters.

The second paragraph describes something important about each one.

The third paragraph describes what happened.

The fourth paragraph describes the characters' hiding place.

Notebook

Make a notebook page like this.

Answers		Leave this column empty
1		
2		
3		
4		
5		
6		

Answer these **questions** from the story of *The Three Robbers* on the notebook page you have made.

1 Which of these words tells what kind of men the villains were?

| pirates | robbers | highwaymen |

Write the correct answer in the first space.

2 What are the names of the weapons carried by the villains?
Write the words in the second space.

3 When did the villains go out?

| in the evening shadows | in a dense fog |
| in the dark of night | in a blinding storm |

Write the correct phrase in the third space.

4 Leave the fourth space empty.

5 Where was the hide-out?

| in a mountain cave | in a deserted warehouse |
| in a haunted house | in a secret island |

Write the correct answer in the fifth space.

6 Which word in the story describes **all** the valuables in the hide-out?

| loot | plunder | booty |

Write the correct answer in the sixth space.

17

Build your own story

In your notebook you have a collection of words and phrases which make the outline of a new story.

Write your own ideas for a story opposite your answers.

1. What kind of villains? How many? Give them names.
   Write a description for each one.

2. Make a list of the weapons used by **your** villains.

3. When did **your** story happen?
   Write some words to describe the weather.

4. In this empty space write notes about what **your** villains did.
   Who were their victims?

5. Where will **your** villains hide their loot?
   Write notes about the hiding place. How was the entrance hidden?

6. What did **your** villains keep in their hide-out?
   What did they use for containers? How were the containers disguised?

	Answers	New ideas
1	Robbers	
2	blunderbuss, pepper thrower, axe	
3	in the dark of night	
4		
5	a mountain cave	
6	Loot	

This collection of ideas now belongs to you.

Writing

Write your own story using your collection of ideas.

Before and after

Have you ever opened a new book in **the middle of the story**, and tried to guess what happened at the beginning?
Imagine that this is the middle page of a picture story book.

While they were doing that another little plant had come up. On its branches were tiny little saucepans and cheese graters and frying pans. It didn't seem to get any bigger, and after a few minutes Lester decided it must be a dwarf General Hardware tree.

Think about what happened **before** the middle page.
Guess who 'they' were and what 'they' were doing.
If this was 'another little plant' what had the first one been like?
What did it have on it?
Perhaps the most important question to ask yourself is:
'What kind of seeds had been planted in the first place?'

Now think about what happened **after** the middle page.
Could a whole row of 'Tree Shops' sprout from the ground?
Make an image, (a picture in your mind), of the whole scene.
Are the goods **For sale**, or would they be **Help yourself**?

Writing

Write a story, in your own way, from the ideas on the page.

Letter writing

A boy in Korea wrote a 'Thank you' letter to someone in this country who had sent him money for new clothes.

He wrote:

*'My thanks that you have sent the money.
I am now become a pair of trousers,
two under-trousers and two warm shirts . . .
I am very happy.'*

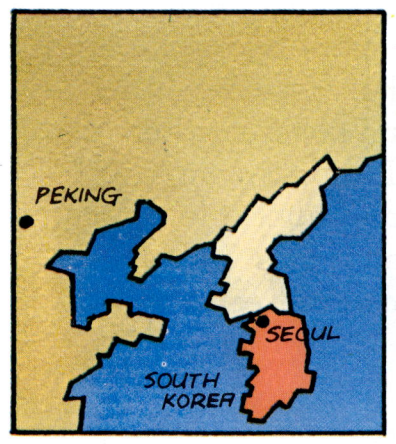

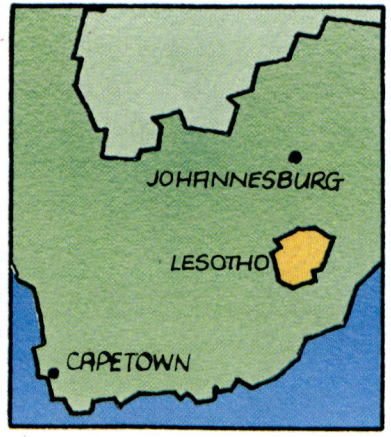

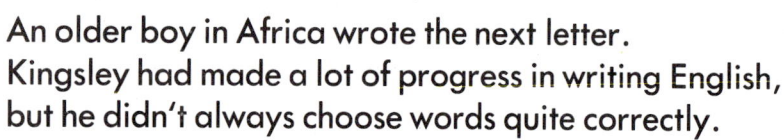

An older boy in Africa wrote the next letter. Kingsley had made a lot of progress in writing English, but he didn't always choose words quite correctly.

*Lesotho,
Africa*

*Kind Friends,
It was to my great surprise when I received some parcel present from you. My gratitude is beyond the utmost reach of human thought and there is no words to express. Could I tabulate the things I bought with it, you would be shocked with pleasure.*

*I have bought by it these are the things: a bag for carrying my school books; books, a blazer and a full school uniform. As I fail to hit on the right verb to express my great thanks I think all my gratitude should be expressed in four words which I think they are not little as far as I am concerned. The great words are —
'thank you very much'.*

*Yours obediently,
Kingsley Salepe*

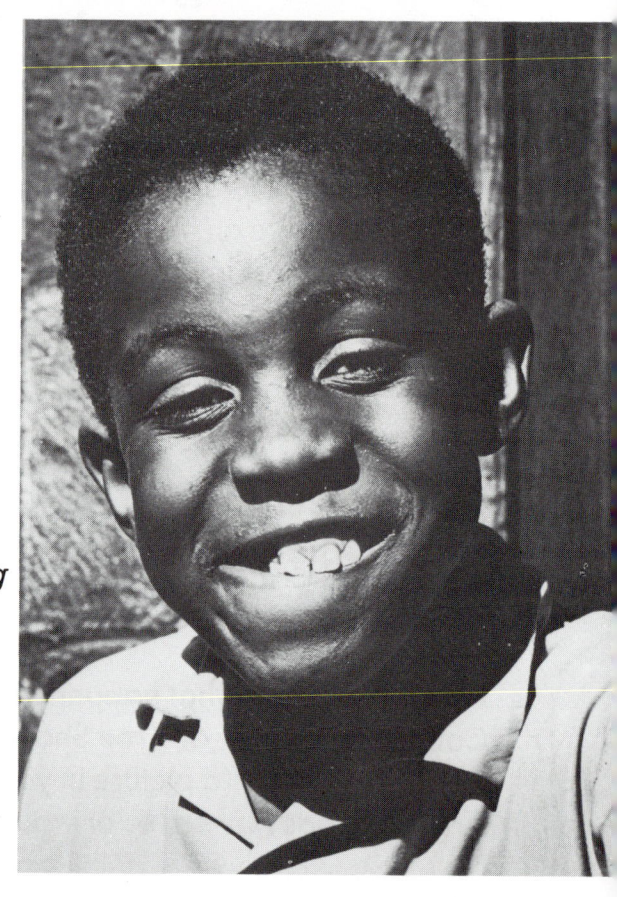

The two letters on page 20 are in a book called *The Friday Miracle* (Puffin), published in aid of The Save the Children Fund.

We often hear about children in other countries who need our help. Sometimes a disaster can leave children without **necessities,** such as food and clothing.
Some children are too poor to enjoy **luxuries,** such as books and writing materials.

Notebook

Make a list of ideas for:

Necessities	and	**Luxuries**
water		television
tools		chocolate

Add more of your own.

You can help to provide children in other countries with **necessities.**
You and your friends can organize ways of raising money to send to The Save the Children Fund.

Make a list of interesting ways of raising money.
You could arrange:
   an entertainment,
   a sale,
   a sponsored . . .
Your teachers/parents may help you.

Writing

When you send your money to The Save the Children Fund, write a letter telling how the money was raised.
Head your paper correctly and write the date underneath.

12 Beech House,
Cresent Way,
Lee,
London S.E.13 5SQ

Your home or school address
District
and Post Code

Smithfield School
Green Street
Brighton
Sussex, EN1 6GQ

Post your letter to this address:

Schools Department
The Save the Children Fund
157 Clapham Road
London, S.W.9 0PT

Remember to write the address clearly.

Pudding time

Do you like Christmas pudding?

Mrs Beaton, who wrote a famous cookery book over 100 years ago, describes this recipe as 'very good'.

600g raisins
200g currants
200g mixed peel
300g fresh breadcrumbs
300g suet
8 eggs

The ingredients have to be stirred together very thoroughly to make a good mix. In some families everyone takes a turn at stirring the pudding. It is traditional that as each person stirs they make a wish.

What would **you** wish for if you were stirring a Christmas pudding?

When the cook was writing down the pudding recipe she put all the full stops in the wrong place. This was the result:

Slice the mixed peel.
With a knife wash the raisins and currants.
And dry mix the suet and breadcrumbs and throw away.
Any eggs which are bad you can add.
A wineglass of brandy (optional) and beat.
All the ingredients together and.
Cook all your guests will enjoy it.

Write

Write: *How to Make a Pudding* with all the full stops in the right places.

Have you ever heard of: *The Magic Pudding* ? This is a traditional story from Australia about a Magic Puddin' which was invented by a ship's cook called Curry-and-Rice. The extraordinary thing about this Magic Puddin' was that whenever its owners wanted a change of food, all they had to do was to whistle twice and turn the basin round.

Steak and Kidney: *whistle twice*
Boiled Jam Roll: *whistle twice*
Apple and Dumpling: *whistle twice* and so on.

In the story, a hungry Koala bear called Bunyip
sees Bill Barnacle and Sam Sawnoff enjoying some of their pudding.

Bill

Sam

Bunyip

'You'll enjoy this Puddin',' said Bill, handing him a large slice.
'This is a very rare puddin'.'
'It's a cut-and-come-again Puddin',' said Sam.
'It's a Christmas steak and apple-dumpling Puddin',' said Bill.
'It's a Magic Puddin' . . .'

. . . All three had a delightful meal, eating as much as possible,
for whenever they stopped eating the Puddin' sang out —
'Eat away, chew away, munch and bolt and guzzle.
Never leave the table till you're full up to the muzzle . . .'

The peculiar thing about the Puddin' was that, although they all
had a great many slices off him, there was no sign of the place
whence the slices had been cut. 'That's where the magic comes in,'
explained Bill. 'The more you eats the more you gets.
Cut-and-come-again is his name and cut-and-come-again is his nature.
Me an' Sam has been eatin' away at this Puddin' for years,
and there's not a mark on him.'

Imagine owning a pudding which could never be eaten up.
Imagine owning a pudding which could be changed to any flavour.
Imagine the number of people who would try to borrow it!

Write

Write a story about: *A Magic Pudding*

Other ideas

Did you know that:

Ham and **Sandwich**
are places in Kent

Fry Up
is in Yorkshire

Water of Milk
is a River in Scotland

You could make your own collection of: *Extraordinary Food Facts*

What's inside?

wallet

beach bag

waste paper basket

jewel box

shopping basket

suitcase

| torn envelope | cabbage | bedroom slippers | £5 note |
| swimming trunks | ruby ring | | |

Match each item in the box with the container in which you are most likely to find it.

Think about a very special container, a **Christmas stocking**.

When Susan Garland pinched her stocking from top to toe on Christmas morning:

It was full of nice knobs and lumps, a fat thing like a book stuck out of the top. She drew it out. She ran her fingers along like a blind man and could not read the title, but there were words on it. Next came an apple with its sweet, sharp odour. Next came a curious thing, painted and spiked, with battlements like a tower. Whatever could it be? It was smooth like ivory and shone even in the dark. She ran her fingers round the little rim and found a knob. She gave it a tug, and a ribbon flew out — it was a tape measure to measure a thousand things.

Write

Write a short piece about opening a Christmas stocking in the dark on Christmas morning.
Describe the shapes as you run your fingers round the knobs and bumps.
You could guess what each one is before you identify it.
You could call your writing: *Finger Pleasures*

Think about **pockets**.

When Tom Sawyer emptied his pocket he had:

twelve marbles, part of a jew's harp, a piece of blue bottle-glass to look through, a spool cannon, a key that wouldn't unlock anything, a fragment of chalk, a glass stopper of a decanter, a tin soldier, a couple of tadpoles, six fire-crackers, a brass door knob, a dog collar, but no dog, the handle of a knife, four pieces of orange peel, and a delapidated old window sash.

Tom often sat day-dreaming, turning his treasures over and over in his fingers and over and over in his mind.

When he fingered the dog collar he thought about . . .

When he fingered the brass door knob he thought about . . .

Write

Write about: *Tom's Thoughts* as he fingered his treasures.

A poem by R. S. Thomas begins:

Look at this village boy, his head is stuffed
With all the nests he knows, his pockets with flowers,
Snail-shells and bits of glass, the fruit of hours
Spent in the fields . . .

How do *you* spend your out-of-school hours?

Where do you go?

What do you see and hear?

What kind of thoughts are stuffed inside your head?

Writing

Write: *My Head is Stuffed with* . . .

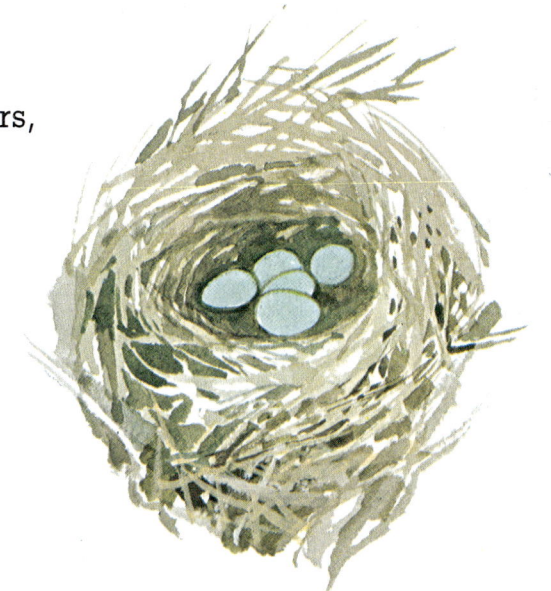

Read this information about two creatures which have **pouches.**

When the baby kangaroo leaves the inside of its mother's body it is small, pink and blind. The body is only half developed and the hind legs are crossed over each other. The new born baby climbs up through the soft fur to its mother's pouch, using its front legs. This little journey takes about ten minutes.

Inside the pouch it is warm and furry. The half-grown kangaroo baby searches for its mother's teat and a drink of milk. When it is properly grown the young kangaroo leaves its mother's pouch and feeds on grass.

When the jelly-like eggs leave the inside of the mother's body they are tiny half-developed sea horses. When she is ready, the female sea horse swims close to the male's body and pushes the eggs into his pouch. Then she swims away.

The opening in the male's pouch closes and the eggs rest in the soft walls of the pouch. Inside the pouch the eggs begin to develop.

When they are properly grown the young sea horses jerk their way out of the father's pouch and swim away amongst the sea weed.

Notebook

Look at this:

Collection box of information for the Sea Horse
baby's appearance   tiny, jelly-like eggs half-developed   **how it gets to new home**   female pushes eggs into male pouch   **father's or mother's pouch**   father's pouch   **inside pouch**   rests in soft wall   begins to grow and develop   **when grown**   jerk their way out   swim amongst sea weed

Make your own:

Collection box of information for the Kangaroo
baby's appearance   **how it gets to new home**   **father's or mother's pouch**   **inside pouch**   **when grown**

Before you write

Think about what is the **same** during the early life of the babies of the sea horse and the kangaroo.
Both babies leave their mother's body before they are properly developed and go and live in a pouch.

Think about what is **different** during the early life of the two creatures.
The half developed sea horse baby lives in its father's pouch, but the half developed kangaroo lives in its mother's pouch.

Write

Write about: *The Early Lives of the Kangaroo and the Sea Horse*
      or: *In a Parent's Pouch*

Using your eyes

As you study this **picture map** of a **landscape**, notice all the **'landmarks'**.

Put your finger on the **Starting Point.**
Now find the **Farm.**
Which way would you go if you were walking from the Starting Point to the Farm?
Would you begin by going over the Stile or through the Gate?

When you give someone instructions for a route, you need to tell them all the **landmarks** they will see on the way.

Write

Write a short piece giving instructions for travelling:
From the Starting Point to the Farm
Write a longer piece giving instructions for:
How to reach the Ruined Castle or: *The Way to the Old Windmill*

As you study this picture, think of it in three parts.

The background

The middle ground

The foreground

The background
How many different games can you see in this part of the picture?
Can you spot the boy climbing a tree?

The middle ground
How many different games can you see in this part of the picture?
How many children are pretending to have a wedding?

The foreground
How many different games can you spot in this part of the picture?
Can you see the percussion band group?

This is part of a famous painting called *Children's Games* which was painted in the 16th century by Pieter Bruegel.
The complete painting by Bruegel shows children playing 80 different games. How many are shown in this part of the picture?

Write

Write a description of the picture called: *Children's Games*
You could plan your writing in **three paragraphs.**
Describe each game in detail. Try to guess what the toys are made of.

Other ideas

Make a list of modern games. Can you think of **80** different games?

Picture poems

A picture can be made for a poem.

Dragonfly

The face of the dragonfly
is practically nothing
BUT EYES.

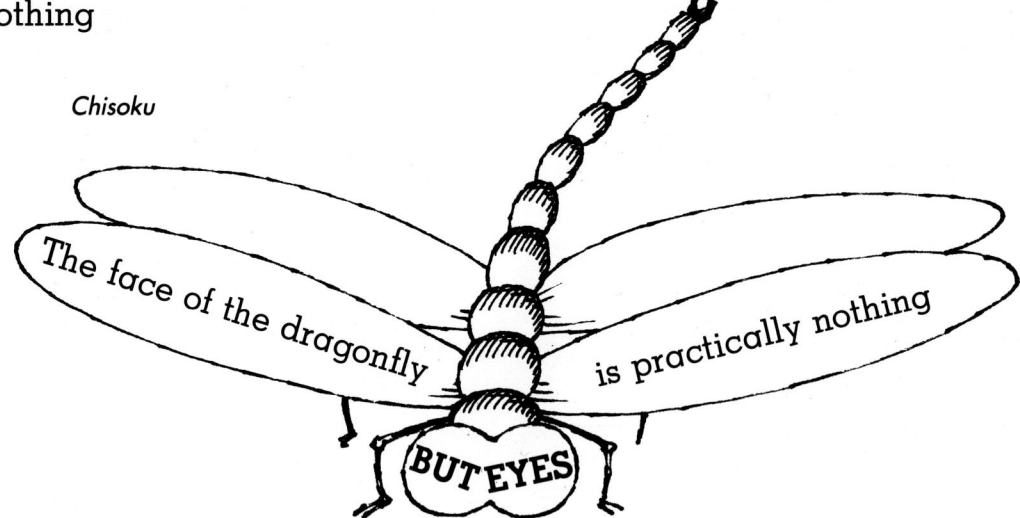

Chisoku

Make pictures for these poems.

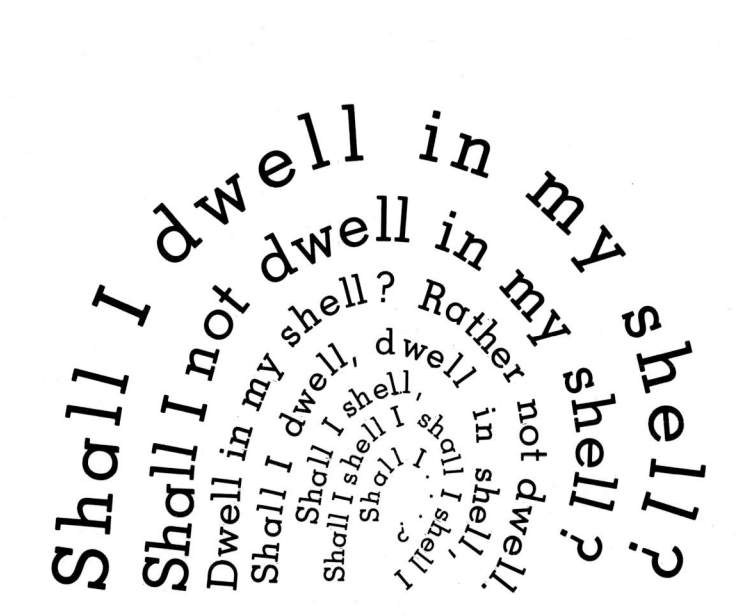

Swinging from trees
like a flying trapeze
with a tail that can curl like the rope cowboys twirl

Christian Morgenstern

Shall I dwell in my shell?
Shall I not dwell in my shell?
Dwell in my shell? Rather not dwell
Shall I dwell, dwell in shell,
Shall I shell, shall I,
Shall I shell,
Shall I.
?

Eve Merriam

D.H. Lawrence made one magical phrase into a beautiful little poem when he described fish as:

'quick little splinters of life'

The Little Fish

The tiny fish enjoy themselves
in the sea.
Quick little splinters of life,
their little lives are fun to them
in the sea.

What kind of word picture or image comes into your mind when you look at this picture?

'Dumb swimmers there among the rocks'

Writing

Write a short poem of your own for this picture.

Write short poems of your own for any of these phrases which seem magical to you.

'a flurry of soft, white flakes . . . falling feathers'
'a shower of arrows'
'a little quaker . . . feet like small leaves'
'a concert of colours'
'the daybreak people are chirping'
'laughing bellies filled with gravel'

Write your own picture poem

Make a picture in your mind of something you know well.
Think of your image in an unusual way.
Write your own picture poem.

Which one would you choose?

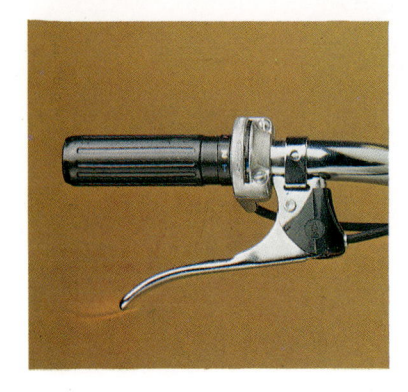

Twist-grip Gear control. Take your choice of gear without moving hands from the handlebar.

THE RALEIGH COMMANDO

is everything the name implies. It's a go-anywhere adventure bike that's really safe for 7-11 year olds. It's even a favourite with the girls too. The 18" wheels have heavily studded tread tyres for sure-grip. The 3-speed hub gear is controlled by the handlebar twist-grip. The powerful caliper brakes have closed end brake shoes. Wide mudguards and protective chainguard are in scratch-resistant chrome. The giant reflector is mounted behind the useful chrome rear carrier and the kick-down prop-stand makes parking so simple.

THE RALEIGH POPPY

For the young ones — an easy-to-ride small-wheel cycle with big play appeal. Quick adjusting saddle and handlebar heights, to suit a wide age group. Deep mudguards, 356mm/(14") pneumatic tyres. The quarter-rise handlebars allow perfect control and the Raleigh caliper brakes ensure safe stopping. A very useful accessory is the holdall with shoulder strap, in denim-look material. Colour finish for this bright little model is Hot Red, with 'Poppy' graphic scheme.

Making a choice

Read the information about the **Raleigh Commando** bicycle.
Close your eyes for a moment and try to remember one very important sentence about the Raleigh Commando.

Notebook

Write the heading: *Raleigh Commando*
Copy the sentence you were thinking about when your eyes were closed.

Write these sentence beginnings, leaving spaces for the information:

> The tyres are . . .
> The brakes are . . .
> The special features which appeal to me are . . .
> (Remember to look at the small inset picture)

Read the information on page 32 about the **Raleigh Commando** bicycle again, then fill in the spaces in your notebook.

Read the information about the **Raleigh Poppy** bicycle.
Close your eyes as before, and try to remember one very important sentence.

Notebook

Write the heading: *Raleigh Poppy*
Copy the sentence you were thinking about when your eyes were closed.

Write the three sentence beginnings as you did for the Raleigh Commando.

Fill in the information from page 32 about the Raleigh Poppy.

Read both sets of notes carefully.

Study the pictures on page 32 again in great detail.

Read the information again.

Write: I would choose the . . . bicycle for myself because . . .

Imagine that you are able to enter a competition
in which there is a First Prize of: **THE BICYCLE OF YOUR CHOICE**

Notebook

Make a copy of this entry form and fill in the details asked for:

All you have to do to win YOUR dream bicycle
is to write the following in order of importance to the buyer of a new bicycle

- ★ safe and reliable brakes
- ★ adjustable saddle
- ★ choice of colour
- ★ good tyres
- ★ twist grip gear control
- ★ prop stand for easy parking
- ★ scratch resistant chrome
- ★ comfortable foam saddle
- ★ holdall for treasures
- ★ protective mudguards

1 _____
2 _____
3 _____
4 _____
5 _____
6 _____
7 _____
8 _____
9 _____
10 _____

Name six useful articles you would keep in your holdall.

1 _____
2 _____
3 _____
4 _____
5 _____
6 _____

I think a good name for a new bicycle would be

(This is my own original idea)

Name _____
Address _____
_____
_____

34

Each of these bicycle parts are described in the advertisement:

gears	brakes	tyres	reflector
prop stand	mudguards	holdall	saddle

Notebook

Complete each descriptive phrase by adding the name of the most suitable bicycle part. (You may need to look at the advertisement again.)

deep, protective _____   twist grip control _____
a giant _____   heavily studded thread _____
a kickdown _____   quick adjusting _____
powerful, reliable _____   a detachable _____

Make a small booklet of about four pages.
Write on important heading on each page. Such as:

Hints on how to use gears
Cleaning
Danger signals
Parking
A drop of oil
Riding at night

Write

Write: *A Book of Helpful Hints for New Bicycle Owners*

Have you read: *The Furious Flycycle* by Jan Wahl?
In this book, Melvin Spitzangle is given a Silver Zephyr bicycle.
An inventor called Professor Mickimecki comes to live nearby.
Professor Mickimecki gave Melvin some little grey pellets
which could turn something ordinary into a 'GENERATING STABILIZING ELECTRO CARBON CONDENSATING ATMOSPHERE PRO-CYCLONIC COMPACT DYNAMIC MAGNET BOX: The Furious Flycycle'.

Writing

Use the idea of: *A Flying Bicycle* for your own story.

Other ideas

What could you do with a motor car which is able to:
fly, change its shape, travel under water, go through solid objects.

The fire bird

These five paragraphs begin the legend of:

The Fire Bird

Prince Ivan was known as the Wanderer. Wise Men warned him of the dangers of roaming beyond the boundaries of his father's kingdom. But young Ivan ignored their advice and continued to roam.

One evening, as the sun was disappearing behind the western mountains, Prince Ivan crossed into the forbidden Land of Shadows. It was here that the terrible demon, Katschei lived.

Suddenly the darkening sky was lit up by a burning ball of fire. Prince Ivan watched in amazement as the gleaming object dipped down over the trees and came to rest upon the rocks. It was the fabulous Fire Bird. Without a thought, Prince Ivan fitted a catapault arrow to his bow and fired.

Unable to move in the catapault's strong grip, The Fire Bird begged the young prince for mercy. 'Let me go,' she pleaded, 'Let me go and I will give you a Power more precious than rubies.' At this, she pulled from her magnificent tail a brilliant fiery feather.
'Take this, the Feather of Power, and flee before it is too late,' she cried.

Prince Ivan unloosed the catapault's string and the beautiful creature flew away, leaving the boy alone in the Land of Shadows. There he stood, in Katschei's kingdom, with only the Power of the Fire Bird's feather for protection.

Notebook

Make a notebook page like this.

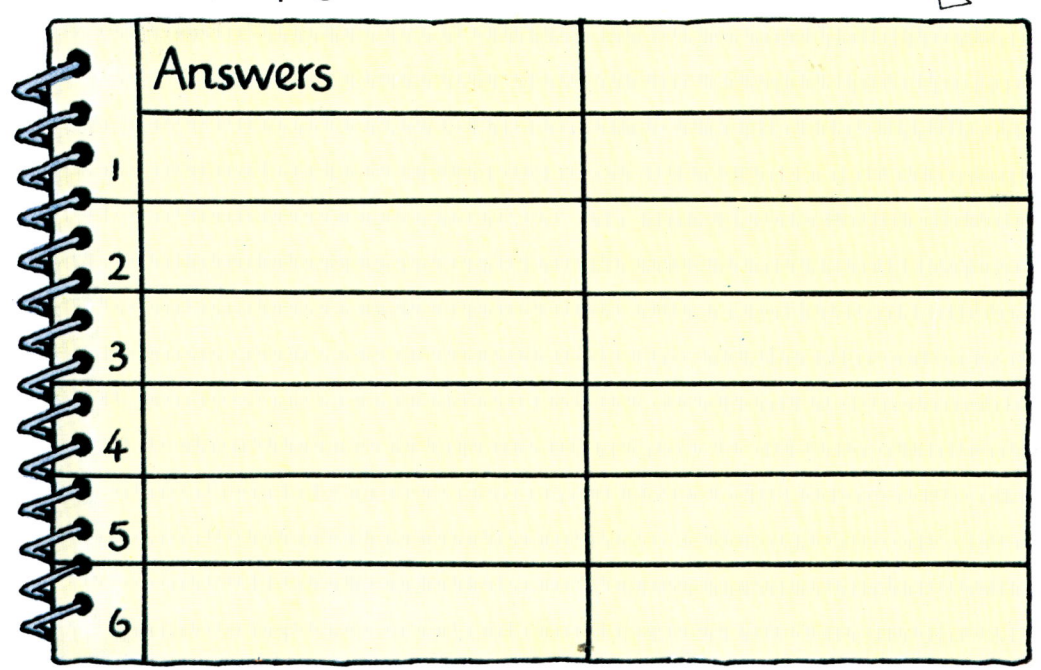

	Answers	
1		
2		
3		
4		
5		
6		

Leave this column empty

Answer these **questions** about *The Fire Bird* on the notebook page you have made.

1 Which of these words is used to describe the chief character in the first paragraph?

| inventor | wanderer | deep sea diver | fisherman |

2 Who lived in the Land of Shadows?

| a crazy scientist | a snake-haired enchantress |
| a terrible demon | an ocean ogre |

3 Who is the important new arrival in the third paragraph?

| the Lady of the Lake | the Fabulous Fire Bird |
| the Mechanical Man | the Sea Horse King |

4 What did the Fire Bird offer Prince Ivan in exchange for her freedom?

| a ray gun | a whalebone harp |
| an invisible cloak | a feather of power |

5 What was the special power of the Fire Bird's feather?

| protection | invisibility | change of size | magical music |

Build your own story

In your notebook you have a collection of words and phrases which make the outline for the **beginning** of a new story. Write your own ideas for a story opposite your answers.

1. What kind of person is **your** chief character?
   Give him or her a name. Where does he or she live?

2. What kind of villain will you invent for your story?
   Give your villain a name. Where does your villain live?

3. What kind of extraordinary creature or person will you bring into your story?
   Write some words to describe this creature or person.

4. What kind of object having special powers will you bring into your story?

5. What will the power or magic of the object be in your story?

	Answers	New ideas
1		
2		
3		
4		
5		
6		

This collection of ideas now belongs to you.

Writing

Write your own story using your collection of ideas.

Fire! Fire!

What a face!

You can see the **shape** of a human head, a human neck and human shoulders, but this picture is not of a human being at all.
Look closely at the eye, the tooth and the hair.
What title would you give this famous picture?

Notebook

Make a list of all the symbols of fire which you can see in the picture.

Make a list of *Uses of Fire* under two headings:

Good uses of fire	**Bad uses of fire**
The cooking of food	The destruction of forests
. . .	. . .

Fire power

Read these two short stories about the **power** of fire.

How Fire Came into the World

In the myths of Ancient Greece the people on earth, who were called mortals, led miserable lives. Then, one day, a giant Titan god called Prometheus, brought the secret of fire power to the earth people. Once the mortals possessed fire they became powerful, because **fire** gave them **power** to do many things. They could cook food, make weapons and protect themselves from wild animals.

In *The Jungle Book,* the chief character is a boy who is brought up in a wolf pack. When the boy cub becomes a man cub, he needs something to give him **power** over the other jungle animals. Bagheera, the panther, tells Mowgli, the mancub, to go to the valley and pick some of The Red Flower which grows outside the men's huts in the twilight of evening. By 'Red Flower' Bagheera the panther meant **fire.** He did not say the word **fire,** because no creature in the jungle dares to call fire by its proper name.

We use the word **fire** in many different ways and as part of many different words.

Notebook

Use your dictionary to make a collection of **fire words.** Such as:

   firelight, _____, _____, _____, _____, _____

Look up the meanings of: fire-water, fire-brand, fire-stone, fire-ship.
Your collection can include **similies.**
Similes compare two things which are alike. For example:

   as hot as _____
   as red as _____

In praise of fire

Hundreds of years ago, St Francis wrote a prayer-poem about the miracles which we can see in the world around us.

St Francis praised:

Our Brother, the Sun,
Our Sister, the Moon,
Our Brother, the Wind,
Our Sister, Water.

When he praised Fire, St Francis wrote:

Praise be my Lord, for our Brother Fire,
through whom Thou givest us light in the darkness;
and he is bright and pleasant
and very mighty and strong.

Notebook

Make a list of ideas about fire as a friend.

> Eg: the cheerful companion
>   the comforter

Make a collection of unusual names for fire.

> Eg: the Red Flower
>   Yellow Fingers

Make chains of words to describe fire.

(warming)—(glowing)—(   )—(   )
(crackling)—(leaping)—(   )—(   )

Writing

Write your own poem about: *Fire*

Other ideas

Write notes about: *Brother Sun, Sister Moon, Brother Wind, Sister Water.*
Write poems using your own ideas.

Tracking and trailing

If you want to direct a friend to a secret hide-out without writing down instructions, you can leave these **trail signs**, using twigs or stones.

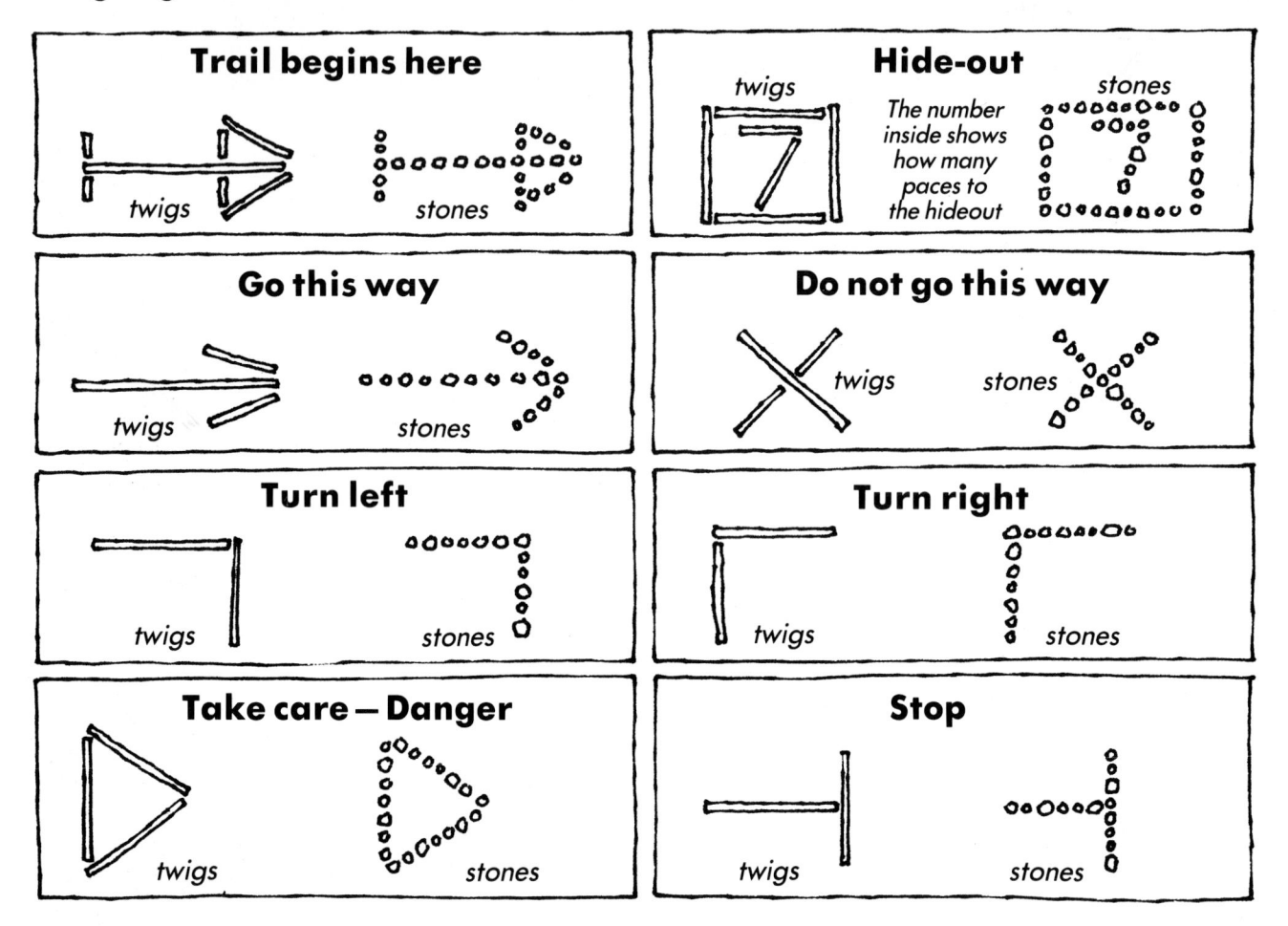

Trail begins here	Hide-out
twigs / stones	twigs / stones — The number inside shows how many paces to the hideout

Go this way	Do not go this way
twigs / stones	twigs / stones

Turn left	Turn right
twigs / stones	twigs / stones

Take care – Danger	Stop
twigs / stones	twigs / stones

Notebook

Write the two secret messages from the instructions given by these signs:

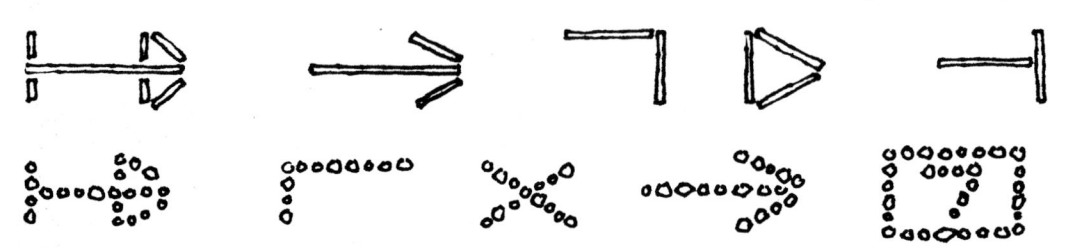

Make up your own secret messages using the signs in the boxes.

Make up trail signs for these messages:

> Beside the gatepost
> Over the bridge
> Under the oak tree
> Behind the church

Suppose you found this plan.
Work out the route to the hide-out, using the trail signs on page 42.

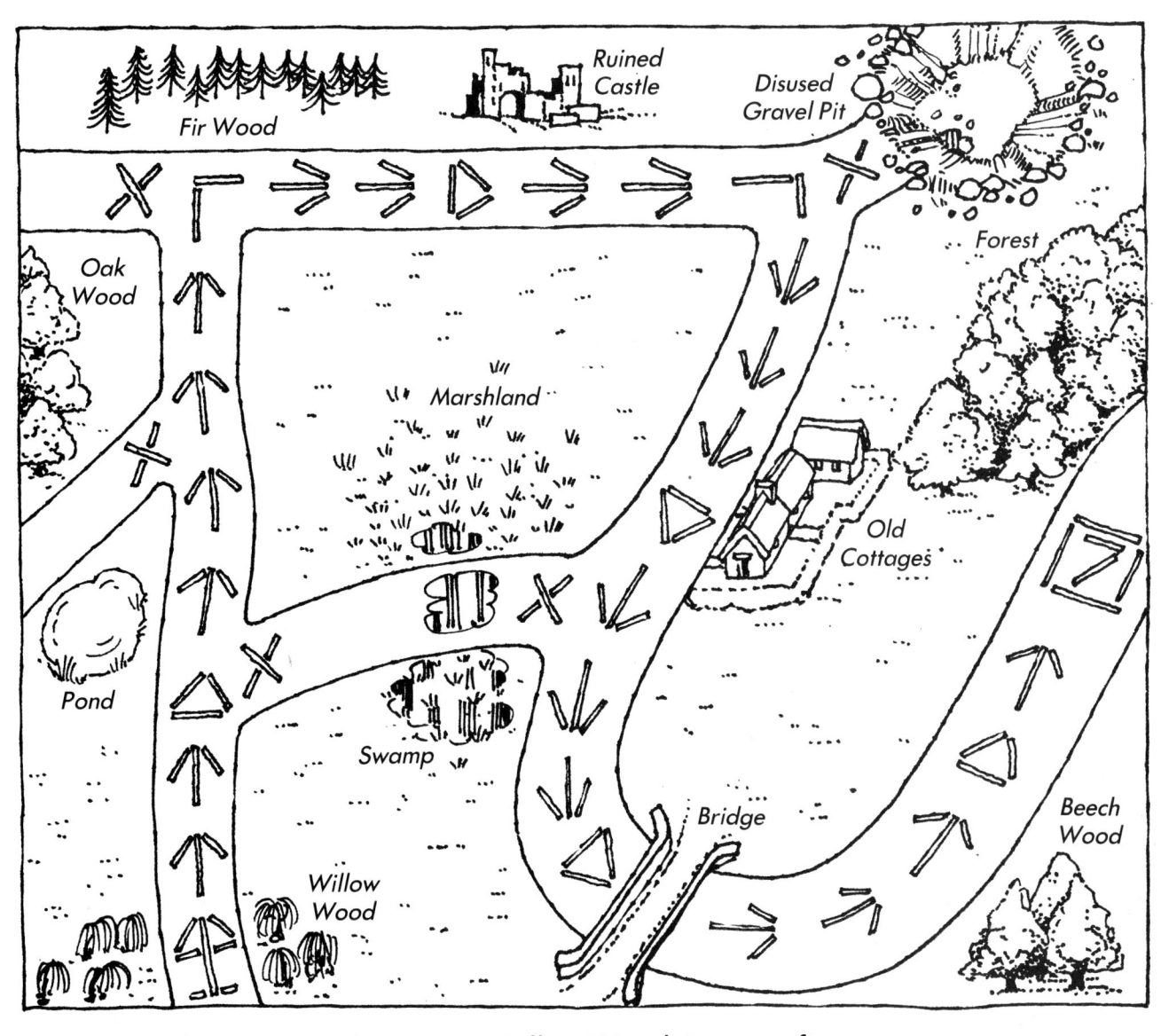

Put your finger on the trail sign near Willow Wood. Let your finger travel along the route. Notice all the trail signs and landmarks.

Think about the false alarms you could have as you travel the route.

What might...
   make your hair stand on end,
   send shivers down your spine,
   turn you to stone,
   fill you with excitement,
   flood you with relief...?

Writing

Write a description of your: *Trail to the Hide-out*

Is the hide-out hidden from view?
Who or what do your find there?

What do you see?

Do you see a tree?
Do you see a hand with fingers? Do you see a foot with toes?

The artist called his picture: *Tree into Hand and Foot*

Notebook

Make a collection of words which can be used to describe the skin
of a hand and foot **and also** the skin or bark of a tree.

> rough   smooth   gnarled   satiny

Now use some of the descriptive words in your collection
to make phrases which compare two things which are alike in some way. For example:

> as rough as the bark of an old tree
> as smooth as a baby's skin

Points of view

Read this description of how different creatures see a bucket of water.

'Everyone should have his point of view...
From here that looks like a bucket of water, but from an ant's point of view it's a vast ocean, from an elephant's just a cool drink, and to a fish, of course, it's home. So, you see, the way you see things depends a great deal on where you look at them from.'

Think about how the members of each of these two groups could see a tree.

Group A	Group B
a woodcarver	a bird
a carpenter	a squirrel
an escaped prisoner	a wood louse
a weary traveller	a giraffe

Write

Write a short piece about how the different people or creatures in each group could see a tree.

Your piece could be a poem called: *Trees are Different to Different People*

More ideas for writing

children on 5th November

newspaper reporters

fireman

wild animals

Ways of looking at fire

long distance lorry driver

children on 25th December

artist

polar bear

Snow views

45

Another point of view

This photographs was taken from **above** Nelson's Column in Trafalgar Square. The camera man is holding a **fish-eye** lens.

The photograph could be called: *Bird's Eye View of Trafalgar Square*

Count the number of people in the camera crew who are standing on the safety platform round Nelson's feet.

Count the people on the statue of Nelson.

Can you count the people standing on the ground far below in the Square?

Imagine that you are standing on the camera crew's platform,
looking down at the people on the ground.
Think of very small creatures with which you can **compare** the tiny figures.
You could make a **comparison** between the tiny figures and ants.
You could say:

  People **as small as ants** move about down below.

This kind of comparison is called a **simile**.

Notebook

Make two lists in your notebook:

Things which *look* small	Things which *are* small
men	midgets
buses	beetles
taxicabs	tin flies
motors	metal fleas
lamp posts	match sticks

Under the first heading write the names of things which **look** small and under the second heading write the names of things which **are** small.

Now write *Simile Sentences* using these ideas. For example:

  The men look as small as midgets.

Write some more *Simile Sentences* of your own.

Read this sentence again: People **as small as ants** move about down below.
Another way to write this sentence is: **Ant people** move about down below.

This kind of comparison is called a **metaphor**.

Notebook

Read your list of *Simile Sentences* again.
Change your *Simile Sentences* into *Metaphor Sentences*.

  Simile Sentence: The men look as small as midgets.
  Metaphor Sentence: Look at the midget men.

Write some more Simile and Metaphor Sentences of your own.

Writing

Write a description called: *Bird's Eye View of Trafalgar Square*
Use some of your comparisons in your writing.

What do you think?

Read this old Celtic story and decide which group of wise men you agree with.

. . . Hundreds of years ago, when King Diarmid ruled as far as the sword could reach, an eagle circled round and round in the sky, and at length alighted on the castle tower. From there it dropped to the castle gate where Diarmid was holding his court. And while all the men watched it in wonder, it placed the egg at the king's feet and then, with a cry, soared away and disappeared. Some of the wise men were of the opinion that the eagle was a bird of ill-omen, and that the egg which it carried in its beak should be crushed forthwith; they said that the egg would bring no good but great evil. Other wise men, however, were of the opinion that the eagle had brought the egg to King Diarmid as the greatest king in the land, and that the egg would bring no evil but great good. And so there was much arguing. But Diarmid, great king as he was, was only a man after all. And it flattered him to think that the egg had been brought to him as the greatest of all kings for him to guard it with all his might. Thus the egg was not crushed, but was placed on a velvet cushion in the king's chamber. There it lay for seven full years. And at the end of the seventh year the egg cracked, and out of it came . . .

Notebook

What do *you* think came out of the egg?
Do you think that the eagle was a bird of ill omen or good fortune?
Write: *My Opinion* in your notebook
Write about what you think came out of the egg and give reasons for your opinion.
Make a collection of **evil** things which could have come out of the egg.

> germs   a poisonous snake

Now make a collection of **good** things which could have come out of the egg.

> hope   a beautiful bird

In the story some wise men were of the opinion that the egg should be destroyed because it was evil. But other wise men had the opposite view and thought that the egg should be guarded because it was good.

Read these: *Opinions of the Wise Men*

The eagle is a bird of ill-omen.
The king should guard the egg with all his might.
The king should destroy the egg.
The egg will bring no good, but great evil.
The eagle is a bird of good fortune.
The egg should be crushed forthwith.
The egg will bring no evil, but great good.
The egg should be placed on a velvet cushion.

Notebook

Find two sentences which are opposite in meaning and write them like this:

First Wise Man   The eagle is a bird of ill omen.
Second Wise Man   The eagle is a bird of good fortune.

Now write the sentences again and add a little more to each one.

First Wise Man   Listen to my warning!
                      The eagle is a bird of ill omen.
Second Wise Man   The mighty eagle is the King of the Air
                      and is a bird of good fortune.

Now find two more sentences which are opposite in meaning and let your two wise men continue their argument.

Writing

Write: *The Argument*

Use your writing from your notebook to start your argument. As your argument goes on, each of your wise men can become stronger in his point of view. They may become angry with each other. When you have used up all the arguments from the story, you can add some more points of view of your own. Ask a friend to read one of the parts aloud while you read the other part of your play.

A great invention

Read these four paragraphs from: *SOS Bobomobile* by Jan Wahl.
As you read, decide whether the boy inventor would use 'the glorious, stupendous, one-and-only Bobomobile' for land, sea or air travel.

One evening early in Autumn, Melvin Spitznagle stepped outside in his wool bathrobe and looked up at the moon. It was a glittering round globe swimming through the tops of tall trees. As he stared at the moon shape Melvin felt a flash of inspiration for his next project. Then and there he drew the first sketch of his new invention.

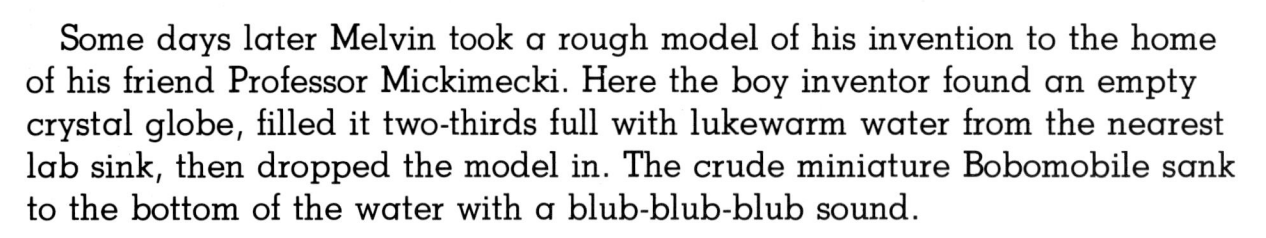

Some days later Melvin took a rough model of his invention to the home of his friend Professor Mickimecki. Here the boy inventor found an empty crystal globe, filled it two-thirds full with lukewarm water from the nearest lab sink, then dropped the model in. The crude miniature Bobomobile sank to the bottom of the water with a blub-blub-blub sound.

After a great many experiments Melvin and the Professor built a full scale finished machine. Inside the Bobomobile were: the controls, the tanks of hot water to heat it, the oxygen tanks, a sea barometer, a search light window, a folding cot for sleeping aboard, cupboards, a library, an ice cream freezer and a tool chest.

Together Melvin and the Professor invented gear and gadgets galore. There was an antisharkbiter, which would bite back at sharks and an Underwater Clothing Immediate Drier. Melvin invented a Bumpus lever. This meant that the wheels could be pulled upward so that if the Bobomobile hit underwater rocks they would simply bounce. The Professor invented a Glub box for recording sounds while the machine was submerged.

Did you guess that the Bobomobile was to be used for an underwater voyage?

Notebook

Sketch out a page like this in your notebook.

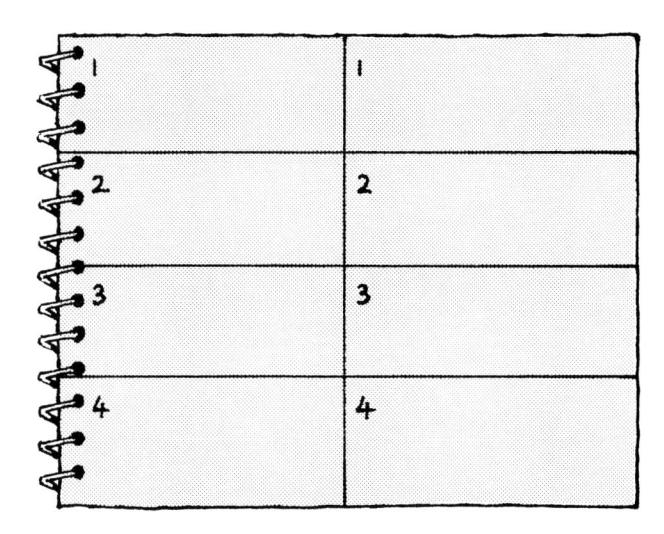

Fill in your notebook page, using these suggestions.

1 Make a rough sketch of Melvin's idea for the underwater Bobomobile.	1 make a rough sketch of **your own idea** for a new invention. Decide whether it will be for land, sea or air travel. Think of a name for **your** transporter and write it under the sketch.
2 Write the phrases from paragraph two of the story which show how Melvin tried out his rough model. took . . . filled . . . found . . . dropped . . .	2 Write notes about how you would try out **your** idea for a transporter.
3 Write the names of the three items from paragraph three which you think were the best ideas.	3 Write notes about three interesting items which you would have inside **your** transporter.
4 Write the full name of the invention from paragraph four which you think would be the most useful for an underwater transporter.	4 Write the name of an invention which you would use for **your** transporter. Write notes about how **your** invention works.

Writing

Using the name of your own transporter as a title, write about **your** invention.
Remember to describe how you first thought of the idea.
Tell how you tried your ideas out and describe all the parts in great detail.

In the book, *SOS Bobomobile*, Melvin and Professor Mickimecki are cruising along, playing soft music when:

In response to the music, a brownish silver-blue rock, the size of a large ice-freezer — now behind them — started following . . . Melvin realized that the rock was in steady pursuit. He let the Bobomobile glide unattended, quietly unpacked a set of Swiss bells, and started ringing them. Then he and Professor Mickimecki harmonized together while the rock advanced, listening. Two very big, interested red-green eyes soon became visible. Next a lengthy, lizardlike tail. Then a frizzy mane and whiskers sticking out about the head. The body, having short, stiff fur, was speckled like tortoiseshell. A rather long neck bent awkwardly to and fro with a rhythm. There were two sets of paddling flippers or feet.
A rain cloud suddenly shot over. The surrounding water now turned brownish-purple.
'She changes colour. Like some chameleon!' whispered the Professor.

Imagine that you are cruising along in your transporter when something extraordinary appears **outside**.

Think of a way to attract the extraordinary being nearer to your craft.

What is very unusual about the extraordinary being?

How can you study this extraordinary being?

Give the fantastic creature a name.

Write

Write a short piece about the appearance and habits of: *Something Extraordinary*

Write a long story

Write a long story about your adventures with your transporter.
You can use the name of your transporter as part of the title.
Use ideas from your two pieces of writing.

Can you solve it?

A cartoon story of: *A Lion with a Big Problem*

On his 21st birthday a big lion called Mr Gronk had an attack of strongness.

He roared so loud that it loosened all the roots of his hairs and they fell out.

A bald lion! Poor Mr Gronk, he now looked like a hairless twit lion.

Lion was heart-broken.

Here are some possible solutions to Lion's problems.

The bald twit lion bribed a hairy ant-eater to sit on his head, but the lion got hick-ups and the hairy ant-eater fell off each time.

He told all the other lions to shave their heads or their legs would drop off. Later all the lions realized they had been spoofed.

Have you got a better solution to Lion's problem?

Make a cartoon

Make a cartoon (a series of pictures) called: *Solutions to Bald Twit Lion's Problems*
You could write a sentence under each picture and use speech balloons and thinking clouds.
Or: You could turn the whole cartoon into a funny story in writing.

Animal lives

Read this information about two mammals who **'see'** in different ways.

The Mole

The mole is a small, sausage-shaped mammal who spends most of its life in the darkness, underground. Its body is covered with thick, velvety fur which almost hides its tiny eyes and ears. Moles have a good sense of hearing, but their eye sight is not well developed. Moles really 'see' with their noses. A mole has a pink, smooth snout like that of a pig. This snout is for smelling and touching. A mole's most important sense is that of touch. On the tip of a mole's snout there are thousands of tiny touch hairs, which send messages back to the mole's brain and help it to find its food. Moles find insects very tasty and they particularly enjoy juicy earthworms.

The Bat

The bat is a small mammal who sleeps in the daytime and then flies about in the dusk of evening. The bat is sometimes called, 'The Flying Mouse', or 'The Umbrella Man'. It flies by stretching out its long fingers so that the skin between the finger bones makes wings. These wings are flapped by muscles in the bat's chest.
When they are flying around at night, bats send out sound waves into the air. When a sound wave meets an object, it sends an echo sound back to the bat's ears. This means that a bat can fly in the dark without touching obstacles. Bats really 'see' with their ears. Their eyes are small and not well developed. A bat's most important sense is that of hearing. Bats search for food in the evening twilight and they have a taste for little insects and juicy fruits.

Notebook

Look at this:

Collection box of information for the Mole
appearance small
sausage shaped
thick, velvety fur
sense of hearing good
sense of sight poor
sense of touch very powerful
tiny touch hairs on snout
sense of taste insects
juicy earthworms

Make your own:

Collection box of information for the Bat
appearance
sense of hearing
sense of sight
sense of touch
sense of taste

Read this poem by Alan Brownjohn, about a mole's life in the darkness.

Mole

To have to be a mole?

It is like, in a way,
being a little car driven
in the very dark,
            owned
by these endless-
ly tunnelling paws and small
eyes that are good, only,
for the under-ground.

What can you know of me, this
warm black engine of
busying velvet?

Mole thinks of himself as a car being driven underground.
How could Bat think of himself?

Writing

Write a poem called: *To Have To Be a Bat*
Collect information about other mammals
and then make a collection of: *To Have To Be*, poems.

Other ideas

You could include: *To Have To Be Me*, and write about yourself.
Do you like being **you**? Think about what you dislike **having** to do.
Write about: *To Have To Be Me*

Read about *The Bat-Poet* by Randell Jarrell

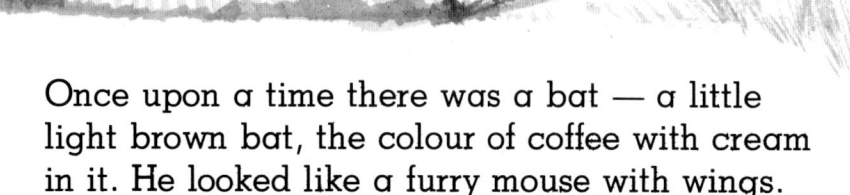

Once upon a time there was a bat — a little
light brown bat, the colour of coffee with cream
in it. He looked like a furry mouse with wings.

This bat was not like other bats — he just
couldn't sleep properly during the day.
As he hung upside-down in the house porch
he kept waking up and looking at the world.
At first the brightness hurt his eyes, but
in time he began to see things differently
from other bats, who from dawn to sunset never
opened their eyes.

One of the first discoveries the little
brown bat made was to find that the world was
full of colours. He made up a poem to explain
colours to the other bats.

Words about the daytime:

At dawn, the sun shines like a million moons
And all the shadows are as bright as moonlight.

The black-and-grey turns green-and-gold-and-blue.

But the other bats refused to listen.
One said: 'What's green-and-gold-and-blue?
When you say things like that we don't know what
you mean.'

Think about how you can describe a colour to someone
who has never seen it.
Compare a colour which you like with a sound, a taste, a smell,
a touch or a feeling.
What colour comes into your mind when you think of:
a hot day,
the touch of ice or frost,
the sound of trickling water?

As you read this poem, decide which lines are a good description of the colour blue.

What is Blue?

Blue is a lake,
A sapphire ring,
You can smell blue
In many a thing:
Lupins and larkspur,
Forget-me-nots too.
And if you listen
You can hear blue
In wind over water
And wherever flax blooms
And when evening steps into
Lonely rooms.

Part of a poem by Mary O'Neill

Writing

Write *Colour Poems* of your own.

As the little brown bat continued to hang upside-down in the house porch, he began to see things differently too.

Would an upside-down bat see a man as a very strange creature?

A bat might say:

Why do you wave your ears in the air?
Where are your wings?
Why do you cover
your smooth, hairless skin,
And wear tufts of hair on your tail?

An idea for a story

Think about a Topsy-Turvey-Upside-Down-World.

How would everything in such a world look?

What might happen to you if your suddenly found yourself in such a place?

Would it be a Delight or a Nightmare?

The naming of plants

STOP!

go...
to the bottom
of the page.*

FLOWER!
the
slowly   slowly
the *petal* curling
the *bud,*
awakening.

Oh, the
up!
straight
I know!
Now
hm
hm
see.   see.
me   Hm   me
Let   Let
higher . . .
must reach
for the sky —
Now, must reach
I be!
I live!
up
tip
warmth
coolness
water,
food and
life growing,
life, being,
in the dark —
(seed style)
spark
A

begin here ⇨

*Read this poem called: *Spring Burst* by John Travers Moore.

Writing

Try to write *An Awakening Poem* like this. Give the plant a name.

58

How did plants get their names?

Old Man's Beard   *Dandelion*   *Buttercup*

Monkey Puzzle   *Sunflower*   *Weeping Willow*

Foxgloves

Do you know this story of how the Forget-me-not got its name?

A handsome prince was riding along by the river bank
with the girl he was soon to marry.
'Look at those pretty blue flowers growing on the
edge of the water,' exclaimed his future bride.
'I wish I had some for my bower.'
'Your wish is my command,' replied the gallant
prince as he leapt down from his horse.
Stretching out his hand to reach the little blooms,
the prince slipped, missed his footing and fell headlong
into the deep water.
Unable to reach the bank again, the prince gave
one last lingering look at his beloved princess, calling
'Forget-me-not! Forget-me-not!'
And with these words on his lips he sank to the
bottom of the river.

Writing

Write a story about how a plant could have got its name.

Other ideas

How many: *Growing Things* can you think of?

| A New Building | You | A Tree | A Tadpole | A... |

Can you make a list containing a hundred different examples?

Strange places

Before Neil Armstrong landed on the moon in 1969, people used their imagination about life there.

The poet Ted Hughes wrote:

Foxgloves on the moon keep to dark caves.
They come out at the dark of the moon only and in waves,
Swarm through the moon-towns and wherever there's a chink
Slip into the houses and spill all the money, clink-clink,
And crumple the notes and re-arrange the silver dishes,
And dip hands into goldfish bowls and stir the goldfish
And thumb the edges of mirrors, and touch the sleepers
Then at once vanish into the far distance with a wild laugh
leaving the house smelling faintly of Virginia Creepers.

Just suppose... that there is a planet, not yet visited by man, where there are:

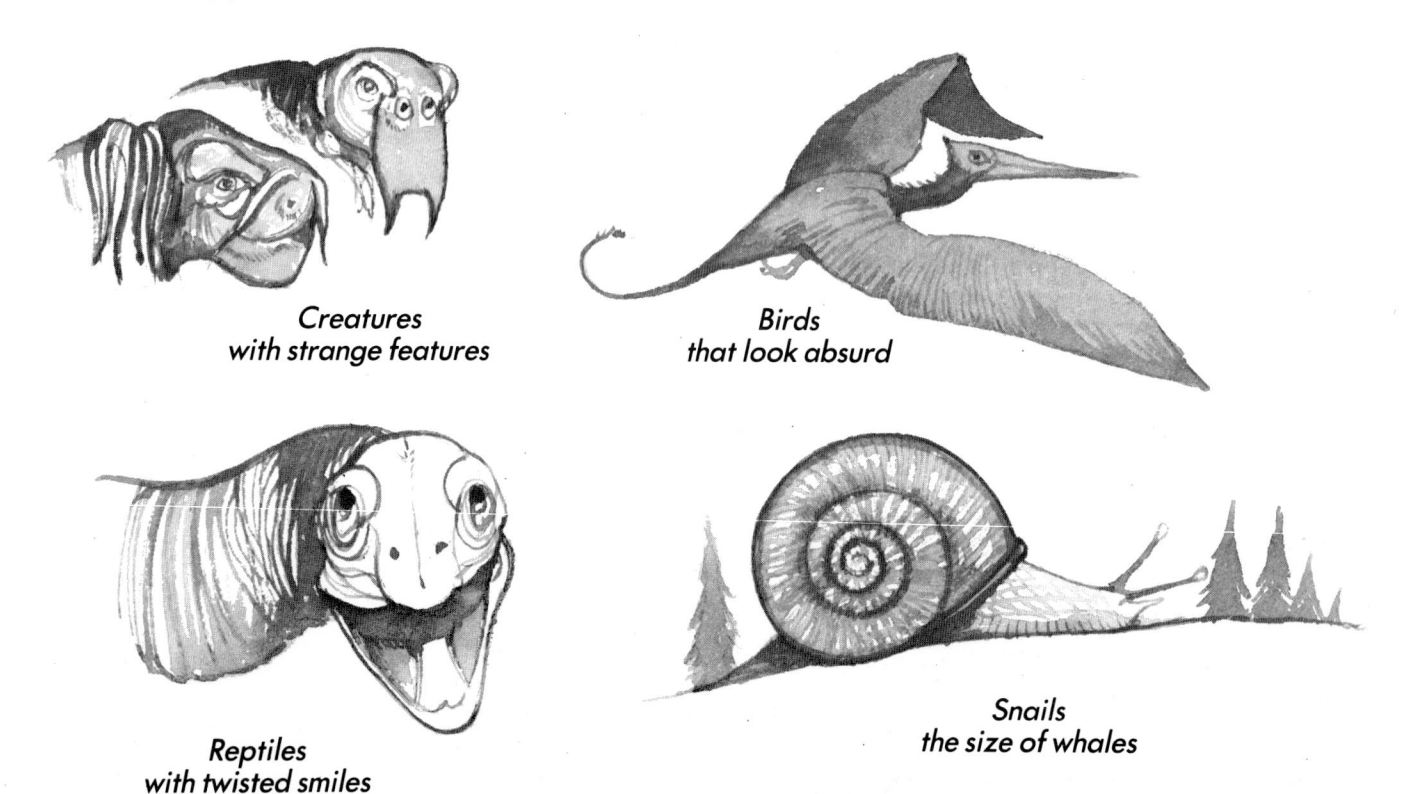

Creatures with strange features

Birds that look absurd

Reptiles with twisted smiles

Snails the size of whales

In his poem: *Foxglove*, Ted Hughes writes about foxgloves as if they are almost human.

Notebook

Write these phrases in the middle of the page, leaving a space on each side.

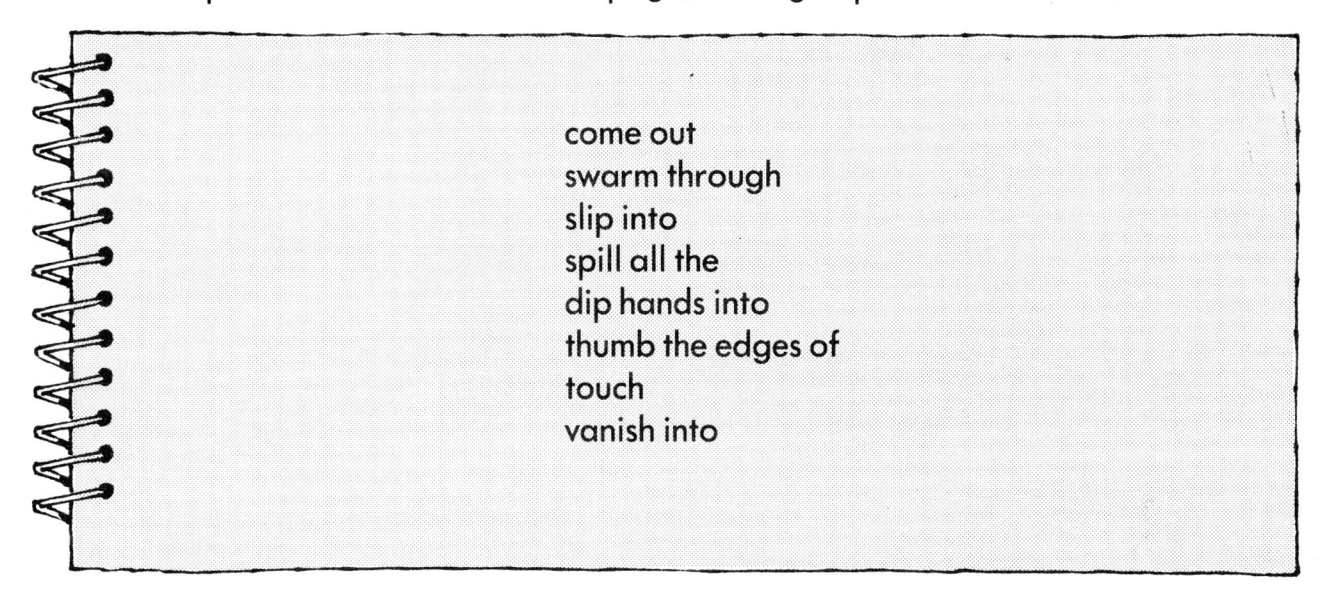

> come out
> swarm through
> slip into
> spill all the
> dip hands into
> thumb the edges of
> touch
> vanish into

At the beginning of each phrase write the name of a different plant or creature.

At the end of each phrase write something weird or strange which each one could do.

Close your eyes and imagine that you are on a strange new planet.

Notebook

Write these **Senses** headings:

> **Smells**   **Tastes**   **Sounds**   **Touches**   **Sights**

Write some of your own ideas under each heading.

Read page 60 again. Read your own notebook ideas again. Change some of your ideas if you can think of better ones.

Writing

Write a description of: *The Strangest Place in The Universe*
This description could become Chapter One of a longer story.

In the second chapter you could *Meet the Inhabitants*.

What will happen in later chapters?

Making a holiday choice

Which holiday would you choose?

English Tourist Board
Activity and hobby holidays

Colony Holidays (DES)
Linden Manor, Upper Colwell, Malvern, Worcestershire WR13 6PP
Tel. Colwall (0684) 40501
Contact: Jane Orton
7, 9 and 12 day children's activity holidays: games, walking; exploring the countryside, singing, dancing, swimming, painting, kite making, collage, macrame, drama, story-telling and reading at about 30 centres throughout the UK, at New Year, Easter, Whitsun and summer.
Price, including accompanied travel, can be obtained from above address.
🐎 Age: 8 to 15. Individuals. Accommodation full board at centre in dormitories

Key

DES This is short for: Department of Education and Science.

🐎 This sign means that children may go on the holiday unaccompanied by an adult.

Langley Children's Holidays
Beaudesert Park School, Minchinhampton, Stroud, Gloucestershire GL5 9AF
Tel. Nailsworth (045 388) 2633
Contact: Mr P.J. Prior, 'Doonside', 22, Manor Road, Romford, Essex RM1 2RA
Tel. Romford (0708) 47112
28 night multi-activity holidays from 28th July to 25th August. Outdoor activities include: horse riding, swimming, soccer, cricket, baseball, rounders, volleyball, badminton, tennis, den-building, making tree huts, treasure trails, camp fires and barbecues. Woods and grassed areas for games. Indoor pastimes include: films, disco, snooker tables, table tennis, chess, draughts, art and craft, TV, gymnasium for games, talent and fancy dress shows.
Two days for an excursion and Stroud Leisure Centre with shopping. Price, including excursions, can be obtained from above address.
Age: 7 to 13. Individuals and groups of up to 20. Accommodation full board at centre in dormitories.

Notebook

Make copies of these two activity sheets.
Write the activities in order of importance to you for **each** holiday.

Colony Holidays		Langley Children's Holidays	
games	1_____	horse riding	1_____
walking and exploring	2_____	swimming	2_____
singing	3_____	ball games	3_____
dancing	4_____	den building	4_____
swimming	5_____	treasure trails	5_____
painting	6_____	films and TV	6_____
craft activities	7_____	disco	7_____
drama	8_____	chess	8_____
story telling	9_____	camp fires and barbecues	9_____
reading	10_____	talent and fancy dress shows	10_____

Read all the information in both advertisements again.
Read your own notebook lists giving the order of importance to you
of the activities.
Which holiday would you choose?
It would probably help if you closed your eyes and tried to remember
the one single activity which attracts you most.

Write

Write a short piece called: *My Holiday Choice*

Other ideas

If you were offered a free holiday in any part of the world,
where would you choose to go? How would you get there?
Do you agree with these travel poster advertisements?

LET THE TRAIN TAKE THE STRAIN

IT'S SAFER BY SEA

TAKE A TAXI

GO BY AIR WITHOUT A CARE

Acknowledgments

For permission to use copyright material acknowledgement is made to the following:

For the extract from **The Magic Pudding** by Norman Lindsay © Janet Glad to the author and reprinted by permission of Angus and Robertson (UK) Ltd; for the photograph of the Korean boy (by Hubertus Kanus), the photograph of the African boy (by Keith Lambert) and the two photographs of fish (top photo by Robert Gumpert) to Barnaby's Picture Library; for the illustration from The Adventures of Lester to Quentin Blake and A.P. Watt and for the extract from the same book to the author and BBC Publication; for the extract from **The Phantom Tollbooth** by Norman Juster to the author and Collins Publishers; for 'Day Dreams' by Richard Crompton to the author; for 'Sailor John' from **The Little Pot Boiler** and 'The Bald Twit Lion' from **A Book of Milliganimals** by Spike Milligan to the author and Dennis Dobson Books Ltd; for the extract from **Borrobil** by William Croft Dickinson to the author and by permission of the executors; for 'Foxgloves' from **The Earth Owl and Other Moon People** by Ted Hughes and for the extract from **The Country Child** by Alison Uttley to the authors and reprinted by permission of Faber and Faber Ltd; for the extract from **Charlie and the Chocolate Factory** by Roald Dahl to the author and George Allen & Unwin (Publishers) Ltd; for the extract from 'Farm Child' from **Song of the Year's Turning** taken from **The Selected Poems of R.S. Thomas** to the author and Granada Publishing Ltd; for the extract from 'Worms and the Wind' from **The Complete Poems of Carl Sandburg,** copyright 1950 by Carl Sandburg, renewed 1978 by Margaret Sandburg, Helga Sandburg Crile and Janet Sandburg. Reprinted by permission of Harcourt Brace Jovanovich; for the haiku 'Dragonfly' by Chisoku from **A History of Haiku,** translated by R.H. Blyth to the author, translator and the Hokuseido Press; for the extract from 'What in the World' by Eve Merriam, copyright © 1962 by Eve Merriam, reprinted by permission of Eve Merriam c/o International Creative Management; for 'Das Feuer' and 'Kinderspiele' (Pieter Bruegel) to the artists and Kunsthistorisches Museum; for 'Little Fish' from **The Complete Poems of D.H. Lawrence** to the author and the estate of the late Mrs. Frieda Lawrence Ravagli and to Laurence Pollinger Ltd; for 'Mole' by Alan Brownjohn from **Brownjohn's Beasts** to the author and by permission of Macmillan, London and Basingstoke; for the extract from **The Three Robbers** by Tomi Ungerer to the author and Methuen Children's Books Ltd; for 'Springhurst' from **There's Motion Everywhere**, copyright 1970 by John Travers Moore and published by Houghton Mifflin Company; all rights now controlled by John Travers Moore and used by permission; for the extract from **Stig of the Dump** by Clive King, published by Kestrel Books and Penguin Books Ltd. to the author, publisher and Murray Pollinger; for 'Returning to his old home' by Otomo Tabito from **The Penguin Books of Japanese Verse,** translated by Geoffrey Bownas and Anthony Thwaite (Penguin Books 1964) copyright © Geoffrey Bownas and Anthony Thwaite 1964, to the author and translator, for the extract from **SOS Bobomobile** by Jan Wahl (Kestrel Books 1975) text copyright © 1973 by Jan Wahl to the author, for the extract from **The Bunyip of Berkeley's Creek** by Jenny Wagner (Longman Young Books/Childerset Pty. Ltd. 1973) copyright © 1973 by Ron Brooks and Childerset Pty. Ltd. to the author, for the extract from **The Furious Flycycle** by Jan Wahl (Longman Young Books) copyright © Jan Wahl 1968 to the author, for the extract from **The Bat Poet** by Randall Jarrell, copyright © 1963, 1964 by Macmillan Publishing Co. Inc. to the authors translators and all reprinted by permission of Penguin Books Ltd; for the photo of 'Nelson's Column Being Cleaned' to Popperfoto; for the pictures of bicycles to T.I. Raleigh Ltd., Nottingham; to 'Save the Children's Fund' for permission to use their name in the 'Letter Writing' unit; for 'The Snail's Monologue' by Christian Morgenstern from **Gallows Songs,** translated by M. Knight to the author, translator and University of California Press; for the extract of signs **The Good Spy Guide: Tracking and Trailing** by Ruth Thomson and Judy Hindley to the author and Usborne Publishing; for 'What is Blue' by Mary O'Neill from **Hailstones and Halibut Bones** to the author and World's Work Ltd; for pictures from the English Tourist Board by David Currey to the photographer and the E.T.B.

Every effort has been made to trace owners of copyright material, but in some cases this has not proved possible. The publishers would be glad to hear from any further copyright owners of material reproduced in **Approaches to Writing and Language** Book 3.